ANGELA P. THOMAS

EGYPTIAN
GODS AND MYTHS

2

Cover illustration
'The Gods and Their Makers',
a painting by Edwin Long, 1878.
(By courtesy of Towneley Hall Art Gallery and Museums,
Burnley Borough Council.)

British Library Cataloguing in Publication Data available.

Published by
SHIRE PUBLICATIONS LTD
Cromwell House, Church Street, Princes Risborough,
Aylesbury, Bucks HP17 9AJ, UK

Series Editor: Barbara Adams

ISBN 0 85263 788 8

First published 1986

Set in 11 point Times and printed in Great Britain by
C. I. Thomas & Sons (Haverfordwest) Ltd,
Press Buildings, Merlins Bridge, Haverfordwest, Dyfed.

Contents

List of illustrations

Chronology

From Murnane, W. J. *The Penguin Guide to Ancient Egypt,* 1983.

Predynastic	before 3050 BC	
Early Dynastic	3050 to 2686 BC	Dynasties I to II
Old Kingdom	2686 to 2181 BC	Dynasties III to VI
First Intermediate Period	2181 to 2040 BC	Dynasties VII to XI
Middle Kingdom	2040 to 1782 BC	Dynasties XI to XII
Second Intermediate Period	1782 to 1570 BC	Dynasties XIII to XVII
New Kingdom	1570 to 1070 BC	Dynasties XVIII to XX
Third Intermediate Period	1070 to 664 BC	Dynasties XXI to XXV
Late Period	664 to 332 BC	Dynasties XXVI to XXXI
Greek and Ptolemaic Period	332 to 30 BC	
Roman Period	30 BC to AD 395	

1. A bronze triad of a divine family with Osiris in the centre, his wife, Isis, on the right and their son, Horus, on the left. Late Period. From Saqqara. (Bolton Museum, A.24.1971.)

1
Of gods and men

Religion was a vital and enduring part of man's life and experience in Egypt, the breath of life itself. External aspects of religion such as temples, statues, reliefs and paintings of the many gods and goddesses, sacred objects, writings and burial customs survive as a unique testimony to that religious experience but its inner meaning and significance are far more intangible.

The relationship between man and the gods was both simple and complex. The growth of beliefs over many centuries, during which new ideas were added to earlier ones but nothing was ever discarded, resulted in what appears to be a mass of confusing and sometimes contradictory elements. The origins of this lay in a religion of local cults which later developed links with each other. To the ancient Egyptian this diversity was easily acceptable, being inherent in divine powers who were approached through a variety of images related to nature and animal and human life.

Therefore in those terms the gods were born, lived and died and yet paradoxically were immortal. They had relationships with each other, the characteristic divine family being a triad of father, mother and child like Osiris, Isis and Horus; Amun, Mut and Khonsu; and Ptah, Sekhmet and Nefertum. The temple was the house of the god, within which dwelt his cult image, usually a statue. The celebration of the temple ritual, based on the form of worship accorded to the sun god Re at Heliopolis, was a dramatisation of the god's daily life. The three main services at dawn, midday and dusk comprised the washing, anointment, adornment with clothing and regalia, and feeding of the deity with offerings. The great festivals represented the god's social life, when he was taken in procession to visit another deity in his house or received such a visit. The procedure was conducted with all due ceremonial and incantations. This maintenance of the divine cults marked an important distinction between the official religion, which they represented, and the religious practices of the majority of Egyptians. The temple could only be entered by the king as the officiant of every god and by the priests, who in practice deputised for the king in the ritual. Ordinary people might at times come to the outer part of a temple and were able to participate in the festival processions. For most Egyptians their local god was probably their major deity, along with the worship of certain popular and more approachable gods.

2. (Above) The temple of Isis at Philae, which has now been moved and rebuilt on Aegilka Island. The structure dates to the Graeco-Roman Period but follows the plan of a characteristic cult temple with its tall pylon gateway towers, columned halls, and the sanctuary at the rear.

3. (Below) A relief scene of the king presenting offerings to the crocodile deity Sobek in the temple of Kom Ombo. Ptolemaic Period.

4. The black granite naos or shrine which housed the cult statue of the god in the sanctuary at the temple of Horus at Edfu. Late Period. In front of the naos is a pedestal on which the sacred barque was placed. The barque was used to carry the statue in festival processions.

In animal, human, emblematic and symbolic imagery the gods were shown in their many forms, which attempted to present facets of the divinity but could not describe his totality. The true whole divine power remained hidden and mysterious and mortal man was unable to see its perfection. This power is well described in a poem to the god Amun-Re, written in the Nineteenth

Dynasty: 'Of mysterious form and gleaming shape, the wondrous god with many forms. All gods make their boast in him, in order to magnify themselves with his beauty, for he is so divine . . . His image is not spread out in books . . . He is too mysterious that his glory should be revealed, too great that men should question concerning him, too powerful that he should be known.'

5. A painted pot with a scene of a Nile boat with oars and cabins, one of which is surmounted by a standard bearing a divine emblem. Late Predynastic Period. From Gerzeh, grave 101. (Petrie Museum, UC.10769.)

2
Nature and anthropomorphic gods

In the Predynastic Period the local communities worshipped their gods mainly in the form of animals. Divine power which inspired fear and awe was thought to be manifested in certain creatures. These might be wild animals who possessed particular strengths and had little contact with man, like the lion, jackal, hawk and crocodile, or might be animals whose usefulness placed them in a special relationship with man, like the cow, ram and cat. Early man in his imperfectly organised society saw in the animal world a distinct order, which was predetermined, changeless and superior and which, therefore, implied a superhuman power. When human society became more developed, achieving an efficient order under one ruler during the First and Second Dynasties, divine power was anthropomorphised and deities began to take human form. Henceforth gods might be depicted in *theriomorphic* or animal form, in *anthropomorphic* or human form, or in a *therianthropic* or hybrid form with human body and animal head. The early animal links were therefore retained either in the god's shape, in the attributes assigned to him, or in his association with certain animals deemed to be sacred to him.

During the Late Predynastic Period each district was recognised by a representation of its main god mounted on a standard or pole, these emblems being shown on some of the painted pottery. In addition to the animal representations, some standards had inanimate symbols, pointing to the worship of other powers. Symbols which have been identified include the thunderbolt cult-sign of Min, a god of fertility and desert paths from Coptos, and the crossed arrows and shield of Neith, a protector goddess from Sais. In the First Dynasty these two deities assumed human form, Min as an ithyphallic figure and Neith as a woman with her weapons. Min and Neith survived into the Dynastic Period but the fate of the other Predynastic local animal and inanimate gods is much less easily traced. Some remained essentially local, some gained a widespread popular recognition, and certain deities rose to national significance. During this process gods worshipped in the same animal eventually fused together, while others retained a separate identity. At different periods for political reasons a local deity might be raised to become a state god, a position which could be temporary or permanent.

The hawk deity as Horus from the Delta was the sky god and god of kingship as Horus and as Haroeris, the elder Horus. He was also a sun god as Harakhty, Horus of the Horizon, and as Horus of Behdet, and was the son of Osiris and Isis as Horus, as Harpocrates the child, and as Harsiesis, son of Isis. The hawk god as Monthu was local to Thebes and became the king's god of warfare in the New Kingdom, when Thebes was the capital. The jackal as Anubis presided over mummification and was lord and protector of cemeteries. The jackal as Wepwawet was the local god of Asyut, but also a god of cemeteries, being associated generally with Anubis and more especially with the cult of Osiris at Abydos. Thoth, who was the ibis and the baboon, was worshipped particularly at Hermopolis in Middle Egypt. He acted as the scribe of the gods, a messenger and a mediator as a divinity of wisdom and was a moon god. Khonsu was also a moon god, who could be depicted as hawk-headed, and was venerated at Thebes as the son of Amun and Mut. Ram deities included Herishef of Heracleopolis, who temporarily became a state god in the Ninth and Tenth Dynasties, and Khnum of Elephantine, the creator with his potter's wheel. The ram was also one of the

6. A relief scene of King Sesostris I before the ithyphallic figure of the god Min. From the temple at Koptos. Twelfth Dynasty. (Petrie Museum, UC.14786.)

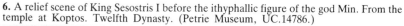

7. (Left) A bronze head of the goddess Neith, local divinity of Sais. Late Period. (Ex-Wellcome Collection, Petrie Museum, UC.8077.)
8. (Right) A bronze statuette of Horus as a hawk or falcon wearing the double crown of Egypt. Late Period. From Saqqara. (Bolton Museum, A.14.1971.)

sacred animals of Amun. Hathor, the cow goddess, had a number of roles as a sky deity, wet-nurse of Horus and the king, protector of the dead at Thebes, patroness of Sinai and its turquoise mines, and divinity of love, joy and dancing with her main cult centre at Dendera.

Amongst the deities who had great popular appeal were Hapy, god of the Nile, a fertile figure with a papyrus plant on his head; Taurt, a hippopotamus goddess, connected with domestic life as the protector of women in childbirth; and Bes, an ugly dwarf often wearing a lion's mane and tail and carrying knives, who was guardian of the home against any evil and helped to ward off danger at the birth of a child.

Some gods, while keeping their usual forms, were also thought

9. (Left) A bronze statuette of Anubis as a jackal-headed human figure. Late Period. (Petrie Museum, UC.8116.)
10. (Right) A faience statuette of Thoth as an ibis-headed man. Late Period. From Memphis. (Petrie Museum, UC.30110.)

to be manifest in a living sacred animal, who was regarded as the *Ba* or power of the god and was a cult image, herald and intermediary. The three best known examples of this were the sacred bulls: Apis, herald of Ptah at Memphis; Mnevis, herald of Re at Heliopolis; and Buchis, herald of Monthu at Armant. In each of these three cases only one animal at a time was sacred, chosen for its special markings, and it could act as an oracle for the god. When the bull died, it was buried with all due ceremony and the next Apis, Mnevis or Buchis was brought forward to take its place.

11. (Left) A bronze statuette of Khonsu with a moon disk on his head, shown as the child of Amun and Mut wearing the sidelock of youth. Late Period. (Petrie Museum, UC.8110.)

12. (Right) A bronze statuette of Khnum as a ram-headed man. Late Period. (Petrie Museum, UC.8152.)

In the Late Period in certain areas this manifestation of a god in a living animal, one which was sacred to him, was extended dramatically. Every animal of the species, in whom the *Ba* of the deity was revealed, was regarded as sacred and therefore protected and accorded due rites of burial. Famous animal cemeteries included those for the cat goddess Bastet at Bubastis, for the crocodile god Sobek at Kom Ombo, for the ibis of Thoth at Abydos, and at Memphis, at Saqqara, there was a great series of cemeteries and underground galleries for cats, ibises, baboons and hawks. This extension of sacredness to a whole species gave

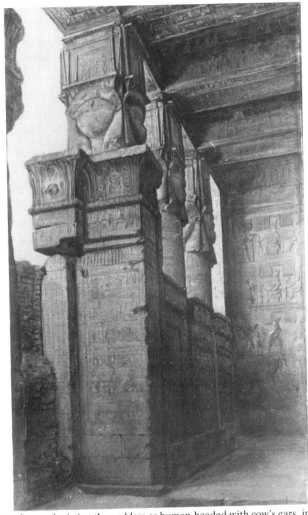

13. Hathor columns depicting the goddess as human-headed with cow's ears, in the temple of Hathor at Dendera. Graeco-Roman Period. Oil painting by John Collier, RA. (Bolton Museum and Art Gallery.)

an opportunity for the ordinary Egyptian to make an offering of the mummified animal image to the god and explains the popularity of these cults in late times. The relationship between divine powers and animals as images thus remains a constant feature throughout Egyptian history.

14. (Above left) A relief of Bes, the protective popular dwarf deity, in the temple of Mut at Karnak. New Kingdom.
15. (Above right) A bronze statuette of Bastet as a cat-headed woman. Late Period. (ex-Wellcome Collection, Petrie Museum, UC.8101.)
16. (Below) A bronze statuette of the Apis bull with sun disk and uraeus on its head, standing on its original wooden sled. Late Period. From Saqqara. (Bolton Museum, A.46.1971.)

17. A painting of the sun god Khepri as a scarab-headed man in the tomb of Queen Nefertari, Valley of the Queens, Thebes. Nineteenth Dynasty. Khepri is seated on a throne and before him stands Isis, who is leading the queen into the god's presence. (From E.W. Butcher, *Things Seen in Egypt,* 1910.)

3
Cosmic gods and intellectual concepts

The cosmic gods presided over the forces of nature in the great natural powers of sun, moon, earth, sky, air and water. As universal gods they formed a higher order of deities, whose cults were more intellectual, inspiring human thoughts about the creation of the world, the order of nature and society, and the meaning of man's life and death. These thoughts, which approached problems from many different angles, were not necessarily expressed in a very intellectual way. They tended to be translated into imagery, an imagery which was presented in human terms. Various thoughts on a particular problem therefore gave rise to a variety of images, which might appear to contradict each other, but which either simply revealed the complexity of the problem or displayed several ways of stating the same answer. In general the cosmic gods were represented in human form, but this was not an absolute rule and in some aspects the god might assume an animal or hybrid shape.

The sun as the source of light, heat and life was worshipped from very early times and from the Second Dynasty became a predominant deity. The natural aspects of the sun were therefore personified in the various forms and names accorded to the sun god. As the creator the sun god was Atum, a primeval deity of Heliopolis, shown as a man, but was also Khepri, the scarab beetle. In the same way that the beetle rolled along its ball of dung, so the sun god was thought to create and push the sun across the sky. The daytime course of the sun was perceived in a number of images. The morning sun was Khepri either as a scarab or a scarab-headed man, and was also Harakhty, Horus of the Horizon, depicted as a falcon or as a falcon-headed man with a sun disk on top of his head. The midday sun was Re, the sun disk itself or a human figure surmounted by a sun disk, or might still appear in the form of Re-Harakhty. The evening sun was later identified with Atum or might be shown as a ram, thus linked to Khnum, the creator god of Elephantine, or to the Ram of Mendes, called the *Ba* or soul of Osiris. In another series of images the sun god was a new-born child at dawn, rising from a lotus flower as Nefertum; he grew to full maturity at midday and became an old and weak man in the evening.

The life of the god was concerned with his journeys. By day for twelve hours he sailed across the sky with the gods in his boat, piloted by his vizier Thoth, the moon, and accompanied by his daugher, Maat, the symbol of his world order. By night for twelve hours in another boat he sailed through the Underworld beneath the earth, bringing his light to the lower darkness. Here he became a dead being and was one with Osiris, ruler of the Underworld, and contended with the region's dangers and its demon-serpents. The final obstacle to his progress was overcome just before sunrise and thus the sun god was reanimated to embark on his morning boat and bring light again to the earth. The place from which he rose and to which he descended at the limits of earth and Underworld was the primeval ocean, from where he had emerged, which was the god Nun, the father of the gods. As creator the sun god had brought into being other cosmic powers, those of air (Shu), earth (Geb) and sky (Nut). The sky goddess as a woman arched over her husband, earth, and, held up by her father, air, gave birth to the sun in the morning and swallowed him in the evening. The sky could also be shown as a cow, an image derived from the fertility goddess worshipped in the Predynastic Period

As a universal god, Re became linked to the cults of other gods, particularly those who were connected with the creative

18. The sphinx at Giza, a portrait of the king Khephren of the Fourth Dynasty. By the New Kingdom the sphinx was regarded as an image of Re-Harakhty, Horus of the Horizon, the morning sun, and was worshipped in a temple built near to the colossal sculpture.

19. (Left) A bronze statuette of Nefertum, child of the sun, who in his anthropomorphic form was depicted as a man with a lotus blossom on his head, often with two vertical plumes rising from the flower. Late Period. (Petrie Museum, UC.8111.)
20. (Right) A bronze statuette of Maat, daughter of Re, and personification of the established divine order. She is shown as a woman with her symbol on her head, the feather of truth and justice. Late Period. (Bolton Museum, A.52.1971.)

process. This is demonstrated by his identification with Amun, as Amun-Re. Amun, 'the hidden one', was an early deity, later described in the creation legend of Hermopolis as a formless god who rose from the primeval ocean. His cult centre was established at Thebes and he was shown as a man with a tall plumed headdress, with the ram and the goose as his sacred animals. As the hidden one, he was the wind and therefore the breath of life. Both the sun and the air as wind were essential to human life and in Amun-Re came together as a coalescence of creative elements. Amun-Re was the supreme state deity of the New Kingdom.

21. A bronze statuette of Amun-Re, god of Thebes and prominent deity of the New Kingdom. His tall plumed headdress incorporates the solar disk. Late Period. (Bolton Museum, 158.1975.)

Political considerations also played a part in the development of the aspects of cosmic gods. This is apparent in the emergence of the physical disk of the sun as Aten, first named as such in the Middle Kingdom, to the status of a great god for a brief period in the Eighteenth Dynasty. As a particular form of Re, the Aten, initially as a hawk-headed god and then in the form of a sun disk with rays terminating in life-giving hands, returned to a more basic idea of the sun's power to offset the growing influence of Amun and re-emphasise the political position of the king. The Pharaoh who elevated the Aten to a state cult and as a sole god, at the same time neglecting the other gods, was Amenophis IV, who changed his name to Akhenaten in honour of the deity. The Aten was at first described as 'the living Re-Harakhty who rejoices in the horizon in his name of Shu (light) who is Aten' and later as 'the living Re, ruler of the Two Horizons, who rejoices in the horizon in his name of Re the father who returns as Aten'. Aten and the king were intricately associated with many shared attributes, thus giving the king an unassailable role as mediator between creator god and man. The ideas embodied within the Aten cult were not new but had always been accepted in conjunction with many other interpretations. Those other features revealed in various divine forms were simply ignored, in particular with relation to Osiris and the afterlife. The Hymn to the Aten, inscribed in officials' tombs at Amarna, Akhenaten's

22. A relief scene of King Akhenaten adoring the Aten as a sun disk with rays terminating in human hands. The king is accompanied by his wife, Queen Nefertiti, and by one of his daughters. Eighteenth Dynasty. From Amarna. (Petrie Museum, UC.401.)

23. A relief scene of Ptah of Memphis with his consort, the lioness goddess, Sekhmet, receiving offerings from the king, Ramesses III, in his mortuary temple at Medinet Habu, Thebes. Twentieth Dynasty.

new capital city, extolled the daytime sun, which left the earth in darkness at night, and there was no mention of the Underworld. Here the afterlife existed in the day, when the Aten brought forth the *Ba* or soul from the body to visit his temple, but at night living and dead merely slept. Atenism foundered on its remoteness and barrenness as a system, for nothing which was so exclusive of other deities could be acceptable. At the end of Akhenaten's reign the old order was restored.

The cosmic gods were explanations of natural elements and firmly fixed in nature. Only one god, who was not solar, was viewed in, before and beyond nature and that was Ptah of Memphis, the most intellectual of all divinities. Shown in human form from the First and Second Dynasties like a primitive statue, he was as Tatenen the earth rising out of infinity and thus in this sense inherent in nature. At the same time, before and beyond nature in infinity, he was the creator carrying everything within himself in his thought and bringing it into being by his spoken word. The role of Ptah might appear to be very definitive, but it offers a particular explanation of existence. To the Egyptian mind the diversity of nature and of human life demanded a range of thoughts to encompass reality.

4
The divine king and deified humans

'What is the King of Upper and Lower Egypt? He is a god by whose dealings one lives, the father and the mother of all men, alone by himself without an equal.' This definition of Egyptian kingship was written in an inscription in the Theban tomb of Rekhmire, vizier of the Eighteenth Dynasty king Tuthmosis III. It comes from a text on the duties of a vizier and was probably copied from a much earlier document.

The central role of the king, frequently called 'the good god' or 'the great god', gave a unique character and stability to Egyptian civilisation. In Egyptian mythology the first ruler had been the god Re, the creator, who brought with him in the person of his daughter, Maat, the concepts of truth, justice and the order of nature and society. Re was succeeded by the other great gods of the Ennead — Shu, god of air; Geb, god of earth; Osiris; Seth; and then Horus. Horus, the falcon or hawk sky god, was thenceforth intimately linked with the kingship and was followed on the throne by a line of demigods called 'Followers of Horus' in Upper and Lower Egypt. When the country was united under one king in about 3100 BC, beginning the First Dynasty, the name of the king was preceded by the title 'Horus' and he was thought to be 'the living Horus' and therefore a god on earth. From the Fourth Dynasty he added the title 'Son of Re' to his names. By the end of the Old Kingdom, with the development of the worship of Osiris, the Horus king became identified with Horus, the son of Osiris. Hence, when he died, he became Osiris, the archetypal dead ruler, and his successor was the next Horus. The successor, therefore, acted as the son Horus in the rites of burying the Osiris as in the legend and was thus recognised as legitimate king. Normally the kingship descended from father to son, but if this was not possible a suitable claimant played the role of Horus in the funeral ceremonies. In certain instances rights to the throne were strengthened by a theory of divine birth, in which a ruler claimed to be the child of a sacred marriage between a god, who had assumed the form of the king, and the queen. Relief scenes depicting these births occur in the New Kingdom temples of Deir el-Bahri and Luxor at Thebes and on the *mammisi* or birth houses of the Graeco-Roman temples at Philae, Edfu and Dendera.

The divine king brought prosperity to his country and therefore his health and power were vital. It is probable that in very early times if his powers weakened a king would be ritually killed. This practice was abandoned before the Dynastic Period but was symbolically retained in the *Heb-sed* or jubilee festival. This was supposed to be celebrated after thirty years of rule and then tended to be held at more frequent intervals. Originally the king demonstrated his physical prowess in certain tests, but later on these feats were no doubt performed by a chosen champion. The ceremonies were designed to renew the king's vitality, to reaffirm his rule and to give an opportunity for all the nomes or districts in the land to reswear allegiance to him.

As a god and therefore able to communicate with all other gods, the king was the high priest of every cult and every temple and the sole officiant in the ritual, and he is shown in this role presenting the offerings in temple reliefs. In practice he could not officiate everywhere in person and would be represented by a priest. In temple services in the morning ritual, after the

24. The *mammisi* or birth house at the Graeco-Roman temple of Hathor at Dendera, which has relief scenes of the king's divine birth. In the foreground are the remains of the temple's sanatorium.

25. A relief scene of Amenophis III, on the left, wearing the jubilee crown, at the time of a *Heb-sed* festival. On the right is the god Osiris. Eighteenth Dynasty. From the temple of Osiris at Abydos. (Bolton Museum, 53.02.7.)

presentation to the god, there occurred a first reversion of the offerings. These were then dedicated to the king and to all past kings in the ritual of royal ancestors, followed by the second reversion to the priests. The king also in theory owned all the land. The crown did possess vast estates but lands were assigned to temples and to individuals. In a barter economy the collection of taxes and distribution of goods by royal officials brought all state functions under the king's control. He was an absolute ruler in a highly centralised administration, but he ruled by Maat, the established divine order.

When the king died, he was thought to join the gods and was particularly associated with Re and Osiris. His body rested in his tomb and his cult was celebrated in his mortuary temple. Some royal mortuary cults were maintained for longer than others and a few kings became the subject of special worship, amongst whom were Amenophis I with his mother queen Ahmose-Nefertari as patron gods of the Theban necropolis, Sesostris III in Nubia, Amenemhat III in the Fayum, Amenophis III at Soleb, and Ramesses II at Abu Simbel and as patron of soldiers in the East Delta.

Certain non-royal persons, all of whom were men who had held official posts, were honoured as gods during the course of Egypt's long history. The earliest and most famous of these deified humans was Imhotep, the chief minister of King Djoser of the

Third Dynasty (about 2670 BC). A statue pedestal of the king found in his tomb complex was also inscribed with Imhotep's name and his titles. He was not only the chief administrator or vizier, but in addition was High Priest of Heliopolis and Superintendent of the king's works. It was in this latter connection as chief architect and sculptor that Imhotep gained fame as the designer of Djoser's tomb, the Step Pyramid at Saqqara, the cemetery area of Memphis. Previous architects had used stone as a building material for certain features in the mud-brick royal mastaba tombs of the First and Second Dynasties. Imhotep, however, created for his king a six-stepped pyramid tomb, which rose to a height of 204 feet (62.2 m) and which was set within a rectangular walled enclosure containing various ritual buildings, the whole funerary complex being constructed with stone. The pyramid is still remarkably well preserved and parts of its complex have been painstakingly restored by the French architect Jean-Philippe Lauer. In ancient times this magnificent monument must have been much admired and it is hardly surprising that Imhotep was remembered as a great man and eventually became a god.

His deification as the patron of craftsmen, but more importantly as a god of wisdom, medicine and healing, had occurred by the Late Period and he was thus identified by the Greeks with their god of medicine, Asclepios. Bronze votive statuettes which were dedicated to him depict Imhotep as a scribe, sitting with an open papyrus roll on his lap. In the Graeco-Roman period he was worshipped at Thebes in the Ptolemaic temple of Deir el-Medina, the village for the craftsmen who had built and decorated the royal tombs of the New Kingdom, and in the sanctuary of the mortuary temple of the Eighteenth Dynasty ruler Hatshepsut at Deir el-Bahri, which had become a centre for healing. At both these places he was associated with Amenhotep, son of Hapu, another deified official. Imhotep had a chapel at the temple of Isis at Philae and was also linked with the Ptolemaic temple of Horus at Edfu, which had replaced a much earlier temple at the site, possibly dating back to the Old Kingdom. It was claimed that the Ptolemaic builders at Edfu in constructing the great girdle wall had followed a design written down by Imhotep. The great girdle wall was decorated and inscribed with the drama of 'The Triumph of Horus over His Enemies', with which Imhotep appears to have become connected. Consequently he is shown as the Chief Lector and narrator of the drama and at the yearly performances of the play was impersonated by a priest.

26. A relief scene of the coronation of King Ptolemy X at the temple of Horus at Edfu, which symbolically reaffirms his rule. Ptolemaic Period. The king is shown wearing the double crown, which has been conferred on him by the goddess of Lower Egypt on the left with the red crown, and the goddess of Upper Egypt on the right with the white crown.

27. A relief scene on a pink granite column from the temple of Herishef at Heracleopolis. Nineteenth Dynasty. Ramesses II, as the officiant in the temple ritual, presents offerings to the god. (Bolton Museum, 14.91.)

The main focus of the cult of Imhotep was, however, at Memphis, at Saqqara where he had a temple, the Asclepeion. Here he was associated with Thoth and could be called 'the image and likeness of Thoth, the learned' or even simply 'Ibis', with reference to Thoth's sacred animal. In the Late Period the vast catacombs for the burial of mummified ibises had been constructed in an area of Third Dynasty officials' mastaba tombs, to the north of the Step Pyramid of Djoser. It is tempting to think that one of these robbed tombs may have been that of Imhotep, buried near to the king he had served. Unfortunately no clear evidence of ownership was found during the 1964-71 excavations carried out by the British Egypt Exploration Society.

Three other officials of the Old Kingdom came to be venerated as gods because they had been wise, good and successful. Kagemni, who was the vizier of the Sixth Dynasty king Teti, was buried in a fine tomb at Saqqara near the pyramid of his king and was revered as a sage. A papyrus of the Middle Kingdom, Papyrus Prisse, recounts 'The Instruction for Kagemni', teachings of wisdom supposedly written for his benefit by his father and which demonstrate that Kagemni was still remembered in the Twelfth Dynasty. Isi, a vizier of the late Fifth and early Sixth Dynasties, became after his retirement the nomarch or provincial governor at Edfu. As he had held the highest office of state the

28. The Step Pyramid at Saqqara, the tomb of King Djoser, designed by Imhotep. Third Dynasty.

Egyptian Gods and Myths

29. A bronze statuette of Imhotep as a seated scribe with a papyrus roll on his lap. Late Period. (Ex-Wellcome Collection, Bolton Museum, 1.1983.19.)

inhabitants of Edfu regarded him as a great man and therefore after his death honoured him as a god, making his tomb a holy place. Heka-ib was governor of Elephantine in the Sixth Dynasty and was buried in a rock tomb at Kubbet el-Hawa at Aswan. He was deified in the Middle Kingdom and a shrine for his cult was built on Elephantine Island. Kagemni, Isi and Heka-ib were, however, essentially local gods and their cults were relatively short-lived. Only two deified humans gained general and lasting recognition, namely Imhotep and Amenhotep, son of Hapu, an Eighteenth Dynasty official.

Amenhotep was born at Athribis in the Delta in the reign of Tuthmosis III. Little is known about his early official career. He was fifty when his rise to prominence began soon after the accession of Amenophis III, whom he was to serve for thirty years before he died at the age of eighty. Possibly he was a friend of the king and was therefore particularly favoured. Although he never held one of the highest posts, being scribe of recruits and overseer of building works, his achievements were greatly appreciated and handsomely rewarded by the king. He was responsible for the constructions ordered by Amenophis III at the temples of Karnak and Luxor and for building a temple at Soleb in Nubia. He supervised the transport and erection of a pair of colossal statues of the king at Karnak and of the two colossal statues, known as the Colossi of Memnon, which were placed at the entrance of Amenophis III's mortuary temple in western Thebes. He also served as the steward of the estates and affairs of Sitamun, the king's eldest daughter.

For these services the king allowed Amenhotep to place statues of himself near to those of his sovereign at the Karnak temple, which was a great honour. The king also gave him a tomb at Thebes, which has not yet been found. His greatest reward was the gift of a mortuary temple, the only one granted to a non-royal person, which was built near to that of the king and which raised

30. The great girdle wall of the temple of Horus at Edfu, of the Ptolemaic Period. The wall was supposedly built according to a design devised by Imhotep.

the deceased Amenhotep to divine status, placing him amongst the cults of kings. By the time of Ramesses IV in the Twentieth Dynasty, Amenhotep was worshipped as a dead king and was thought to be an intermediary between men and gods, particularly in relation to Amun, god of Thebes. He was worshipped mainly at Thebes and at Athribis, his birthplace. By the Ptolemaic Period he had become a god of healing and thus was associated with Imhotep in the Theban temples of Deir el-Medina and Deir el-Bahri.

Although in late times both Imhotep and Amenhotep, son of Hapu, had developed links with higher official cults — Imhotep as son of Ptah, and Amenhotep as son of Apis — they were primarily gods of the people. The great gods were remote and awesome to most ordinary Egyptians, but the appeal of gods like famous kings and deified humans lay in the fact that their qualities could be recognised and understood by everyone.

31. The Colossi of Memnon, statues of Amenophis III, which stood at the entrance of his mortuary temple in Western Thebes, and which were erected there under the supervision of Amenhotep, son of Hapu. Eighteenth Dynasty.

5
Creation legends and myths of Re

Creation legends

Egyptian ideas about the creation of the world developed over a considerable period of time. There appears to be no standard creation myth but a number of versions within which details may vary and which connect the creation with different gods. Certain features are, however, common to each creation legend. In the beginning there was a primeval ocean, the waters of chaos, a nothingness, dark, formless and infinite. The waters nevertheless contained the possibility of life and were personified as Nun, the primordial deity. The creation myths explain how the world emerged from chaos, a world which to the Egyptian comprised a flat earth, a flat sky above it supported by air and an underworld below the earth through which the sun travelled at night.

The Heliopolitan concept of creation was solar, linked with the city of Heliopolis and the sun god, Re. Out of chaos emerged a self-created god, Atum, who was all or nothing, who was the original sun god of Heliopolis and later deemed to be the creative aspect of Re. From himself by spitting or masturbation Atum produced two children, male and female, Shu (air) and Tefnut (moisture). They brought forth a male and a female child, Geb (earth) and Nut (sky). Although at first united, Nut and Geb were then separated by their father for ever, but their initial union gave rise to the births of their four children, two sons, Osiris and Seth, and two daughters, Isis and Nephthys. In later accounts Seth is replaced by Horus or Thoth, although Thoth is never envisaged as part of the family of Osiris. The nine gods emerging from creation formed the Heliopolitan ennead. The system of Heliopolis can be traced back to the Second and Third Dynasties. Its doctrines appear in the early form in the Pyramid Texts, become more complex in the Coffin Texts of the Middle Kingdom and are further developed in the New Kingdom in the Book of the Dead, the Book of Amduat and the Book of Gates.

The Hermopolitan cosmology was linked with the city of Hermopolis and the god Thoth. From the waters of chaos summoned by the voice of Thoth came four primordial gods — Nun, Heh, Ket and Amun — in the form of male frogs representing nothingness, infinity, darkness and formlessness, together with their consorts Naunet, Hehet, Keket and Amunet in the form of four female snakes. These eight deities were the

Hermopolitan ogdoad and appeared on an island rising from chaos. They created an egg from which came forth the sun, who fashioned mankind and gave order to the world. In a variation on this idea the sun was described as being born from an opening lotus flower on the island. The Hermopolitan system is also referred to in the Pyramid Texts. It contains a stage in the creative process before the emergence of the sun and therefore perhaps was formulated before the cult of Re gained widespread recognition in the Fourth Dynasty.

The Memphite theology was linked with the city of Memphis and the god Ptah. In chaos there was one god, Ptah-tenen, who was creator and also the land rising out of chaos. Ptah embodied within himself eight other Ptahs, who had the names of other gods, amongst which Atum was his thought, Horus his heart and Thoth his tongue. Ptah's creation of the world was conceived by the thought of his heart and uttered into reality by his tongue, through the power of his word. The Memphite system represents a high achievement of Egyptian thought and probably had a limited popular appeal, being appreciated mainly by the educated classes. It is a partly early and partly later concept. Ptah was an important god from the First Dynasty, when Memphis became the administrative capital of Egypt. His creative role may thus be a very early one, but could have been instigated to maintain his position later on when the cult of Re was becoming very powerful.

The creation legends with their variations, their later additions and their associations with each other tell the same story, but clearly reflect religious and political struggles. The Heliopolitan concept came to be perhaps the most widely accepted.

Myths of Re
The importance of the solar cult gave rise to a number of myths concerning Re. These emphasised his ritual power as creator, first ruler on earth, protector of the kingship, and giver of light and life on earth by day and in the Underworld by night.

One legend, often called 'The Deliverance of Mankind' or 'The Destruction of Mankind', was inscribed on the largest gilded wooden shrine surrounding the sarcophagus of Tutankhamun and was written on the walls of later New Kingdom royal tombs in the Valley of the Kings, those of Seti I and Ramesses II possessing the most complete texts. At this stage it is evident that the legend was employed as a magical incantation to protect the body of the king and prevent any desecration. The story begins after Re had

32. A relief on pink granite of the air god, Shu, with his symbol, a feather, on his head. Twenty-second Dynasty. From the temple of Bastet at Bubastis. (Bolton Museum, 8.90.)

33. A painted scene of Geb, the earth-god, lying on the ground with the body of Nut, the sky goddess, arched over him. From the wooden plastered and painted anthropoid coffin of Tawuhenut, a priestess of Amun. Twenty-first Dynasty. Probably from Thebes. (Bolton Museum, 69.30.)

created the world and mankind, who came from his tears, and when he was ruling on earth over gods and men in his old age. He became aware that men were scheming against him and therefore summoned a council of gods. The primordial deity, Nun, advised Re to use his powerful Eye, the sun itself and possessor of its own complex mythology, to exact vengeance on the evildoers, and furthermore to send the Eye in the person of Hathor. The goddess Hathor is thus given an uncharacteristic fierce role, but one which she fulfilled with great zeal. She found those who had fled from Re's anger in the desert and killed very many of them, thus gaining the name of Sekhmet, the lioness goddess of war, with whom she is here identified. Re was at first pleased but soon realised that Hathor's delight in killing might lead to the destruction of all mankind, which he had not intended. He hastily ordered large amounts of red ochre to be brought from Elephantine and to be ground to powder by the High Priest of Heliopolis and stirred into seven thousand jugs of beer. The liquid looked very like human blood and was poured at night on to the fields. When Hathor arrived in the morning to continue her killing, she was completely deceived and began to drink. She

34. (Left) A wooden figure of Ptah, depicted as a primitive statue with a close-fitting cap and holding a staff or sceptre. Late Period. From Saqqara. (Bolton Museum, A.24. 1969.)
35. (Right) A bronze statuette of Sekhmet, the lioness goddess of war. Late Period. From Saqqara. (Bolton Museum, A.47.1971.)

soon became very drunk and forgot about mankind, so they were saved from destruction.

This story forms a fairly complete myth of early origin, but in the New Kingdom texts it is followed by various additions, overlaid with some degree of satire, which explain how certain things happened. Hathor's drunkenness was clearly beneficial to men and Re ordered that henceforth festivals honouring Hathor should include drink, an appropriate provision for a goddess usually presiding over music, dancing and love. After saving mankind, Re was still unhappy and felt weak and old. Nun decided that Nut, the sky goddess, in the shape of a cow, should take Re and carry him above the earth, although this meant that he was seen only in the day and the earth became dark at night. In the sky Re made the stars and places for eternal life. Unfortunately Nut began to suffer from vertigo so Re provided pillars to hold her up and instructed Shu, the air, to stand between her and the earth. The problem of the darkness on earth at night while Re was in the Underworld was solved by Re appointing Thoth to give light as the moon.

Another myth preserved in magical papyri emphasised the power of the divine name and was a tale about Isis and Re, usually called 'The Secret Name of Re'. The great sun god had many forms and names, seventy-four of which were listed in the Litany of Re, a text which was inscribed in the entrances of royal tombs of the New Kingdom. He also possessed a true name known only to himself, which contained his potency. In this myth Isis was a woman who longed to increase her magic powers and join the gods in order to rule over them. She decided that the best means to this end was to learn Re's secret name and thereby transfer his power to herself. At this time Re was ruling on earth

36. A faience head of Hathor as a woman with cow's ears. This item was a votive offering dedicated to Hathor as patroness of the turquoise mines at her temple at Serabit El-Khadim, Sinai. New Kingdom. (Bolton Museum, 68.05.42a.)

37. A bronze aegis or protective collar necklace surmounted by the head of Isis and flanked by falcon heads of her son Horus. Late Period. From Saqqara. (Petrie Museum, UC. 30479.)

and lived in his palace at Heliopolis. Every day he went out with his scribe in his boat and stayed for an hour in each of the twelve provinces of his kingdom, ensuring that all was well. He was getting old and Isis noticed that he was slobbering. She collected some of his saliva from the ground and used it to make a serpent. When Re came out on his next daily journey, the serpent lay in his path and bit him. Re fell to the ground, weakened by the poison and in great pain. The gods with him and those whom he summoned were powerless to help him. Isis then arrived and offered to cure Re with her magic but demanded to know his name. Re then described himself as the creator and related his names of Khepri at sunrise, Re at noon and Atum at sunset. Isis persisted in her demand to know his true name and such was Re's pain that he allowed the terrible name to pass from his own body into that of Isis. In so doing he permitted Isis to reveal the name to her son Horus but ordered that it must not be told to anyone else. Isis then cured Re by reciting a spell and with her new power became one of the mightiest of goddesses. At the same time it is implied that when Re takes his eternal position in the sky, the power of his name will remain on earth, invested in the living Horus, the king.

A further story, which is referred to in the Book of the Dead, the Book of Amduat and other texts, concerns the struggles of Re against his principal enemy, Apophis, the serpent symbol of darkness. Apophis attacked the boat of Re at sunrise and sunset and had to be defeated to enable the sun to continue his daily and nightly journeys. In some texts Apophis was overthrown by the magic of the gods, but in the Book of the Dead, chapter 39, Seth played the chief part in a battle at sunrise. Amongst his roles, Seth was a god of wind and storms and was also placed at the prow of the sun's boat to avert danger. The battle was a mainly verbal one, involving various threats, some goading and general abuse. In the end Seth killed Apophis, whose blood was thought to be seen in the red or pink tint of the morning and evening sky. However, wind and storms might also upset Re's boat, so having fulfilled his purpose Seth was chased away and the solar barque sailed majestically onwards.

6
The myth of Osiris

The origins of Osiris are shrouded in mystery but in early times he was a fertility god, whose death and rebirth were connected with the cycle of the agricultural year. Death came to the land when it was flooded annually by the river Nile. After the flood had subsided the new seed was sown in the dark fertile soil, representing burial and the realm of the dead. The germination of the seed and the growth of the crop symbolised the resurrection. Osiris retained this role as a fertility god but soon added other elements to his character. At Busiris in the Delta he supplanted the ancient royal god Anedjety and took his insignia of rule, the crook and the flail. Osiris thus became closely linked with the kingship and Busiris was established as one of his major cult centres. At Abydos in Upper Egypt he absorbed the characteristics of the deity Khentamentiu, Lord of the Westerners, an ancient god of cemeteries, and became the ruler and god of the dead, and Abydos developed into another great centre for Osiris worship. At the end of the Old Kingdom in the Pyramid Texts Osiris is revealed as a complex deity who has formed relationships with other important gods and goddesses and who is the subject of a popular myth.

The myth of Osiris must have been told and retold to eager audiences over many centuries and in many different ways. No doubt there were also a number of written versions of the story. However, no complete account has been preserved in an Egyptian text, although plenty of references and additional and varying details are found in Egyptian religious writings and monumental inscriptions. The only text of the whole legend which exists is that written by the Greek author Plutarch in the first century AD, titled *De Iside*. Plutarch clearly presents a late form of the myth with some Greek influences but provides a very useful story outline.

Osiris is described as the great-grandson of Re, grandson of Shu, and first son of Geb and Nut. In due course he succeeded his father as king in Egypt, marrying his sister Isis. The earthly rule of Osiris was that of a just and wise king, who organised the agricultural, religious and secular life of his people, and who also concerned himself with peaceful foreign conquest, ably assisted by Isis, by his vizier Thoth, and by his officials Anubis and Wepwawet. This happy state of affairs was soon to be destroyed,

38. (Left) A bronze statue of Osiris, a finely detailed and dignified figure of the god, from Abydos, tomb 250, excavated by John Garstang in 1907. New Kingdom. Osiris is depicted in his characteristic form as a mummiform figure, holding the crook and flail and wearing the Atef crown, the white crown with plumes, horns and uraei. As a dead king and god he also has a false beard. (Ex-Viscount Leverhulme Collection, on loan to Bolton Museum, A.122.1968, courtesy of the Lady Lever Art Gallery, Port Sunlight.)
39. (Right) A bronze statuette of Isis with her infant son Horus on her lap. Late Period. From Saqqara. (Bolton Museum, A.13.1969.)

for Seth, the younger brother of Osiris, was jealous of Osiris's power and prestige and determined to seize the throne for himself. When Osiris returned to Egypt from travels abroad, Seth invited him to a banquet, at which his seventy-two accomplices were also present. During the festivities a beautifully decorated casket was brought into the hall and much admired by everyone. Seth promised that the casket would be given to the person who fitted inside it perfectly. The casket had been specially made to the measurements of Osiris and when it was his turn to get inside it was exactly right for him. Seth and his followers quickly grasped their opportunity and immediately closed the lid and fastened it securely. The casket was cast into the river Nile nearby in the hope that it would be carried down by the river and finally out into the Mediterranean Sea to be lost for ever. This did happen but not quite as Seth intended as the casket was washed ashore near the city of Byblos on the Syrian coast, close to the base of a young tamarisk tree, which quickly grew to enclose the casket inside its trunk. The fine tree was soon noticed by the king of Byblos, who ordered it to be cut down and made into a column to support the hall roof in his palace.

Meanwhile in Egypt Isis had heard what Seth had done to her husband and in great distress she set out to find him. Eventually she came to Byblos and succeeded in having the palace column removed and thus was able to retrieve the casket and take it back to Egypt, where she hid it in the marshes of the Delta. Osiris was dead, but Isis had great magical powers and she had the body of her husband. However, one night Isis had left the casket unattended and by chance when out hunting Seth discovered it. He decided to destroy his brother's body permanently and therefore cut it up into fourteen pieces, which he distributed far and wide throughout Egypt. Isis soon became aware of this outrage and travelled all over the country searching for the pieces of the body. She was helped in her search by her sister Nephthys, the wife of Seth, who could not condone his action. Gradually the pieces of the body were found. Egyptian references maintain that the whole body was recovered, but Plutarch says that the penis had been eaten by a Nile fish and through her magic Isis had to create a substitute. According to certain texts Isis and Nephthys

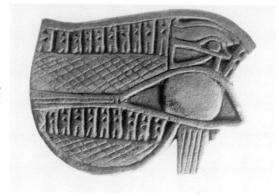

40. A faience Eye of Horus. Late Period. During his battles with Seth, Horus lost his left eye, which was the moon, the right eye being the sun. The Eye of Horus became a powerful amulet as a protection against evil. (Petrie Museum, UC.8817.)

buried each part of the body in the place where they found it, which would explain the number of sites in Egypt associated with the burial of Osiris. In other versions Isis collected the parts of the body and rejoined them to create a mummy, performing rites which gave the dead Osiris eternal life. In Plutarch's account Isis had already given birth to her son Horus, but Egyptian sources relate that she conceived the child from her husband's dead body.

The resurrected Osiris had no further part to play on earth, and as the immortal dead king he became the ruler of the dead. Although Osiris is no longer a direct participant and has had an essentially passive role in the drama, the story continues with the legends of the early life and later struggles of his son Horus, destined to avenge Osiris and regain his throne. Horus was born secretly in the Delta marshes, hidden and protected by Isis. Various dangers, such as snakes and scorpions, threatened him, but with the magic of the gods to cure him from a poisoned bite and with the marsh dwellers helping to watch over him, Horus grew to manhood and set out to do battle for his rightful inheritance with his uncle, Seth.

The conflicts of Horus and Seth formed an epic struggle with a great many episodes, during the course of which neither god escaped injury, but Horus achieved the final victory in this triumph of good over evil. 'The Triumph of Horus over his Enemies' is shown in relief scenes with inscriptions on the inner face of the great girdle wall of the Ptolemaic temple of Horus at Edfu. The inscriptions were copied from texts on papyri and certainly date back to the New Kingdom but are probably based on much earlier writings, perhaps as early as the Third Dynasty. The Edfu inscriptions and scenes are a religious drama, which was acted each year outside the temple by its staff, who played the roles and chorus before a crowd of spectators.

The Contendings of Horus and Seth are also related in a literary papyrus of the New Kingdom, Chester Beatty Papyri number 1. Seth had been defeated by Horus but took legal action to establish his claim to the throne of Osiris by bringing his case before the nine gods of Heliopolis. His lawsuit against Horus, which is narrated in the papyrus, is entertaining and satirical as the gods display very human traits. It appears that the case had been in progress before the Heliopolitan Divine Council for eighty years and the gods were understandably becoming impatient and short-tempered, yet they seemed unable to decide upon a judgement. The case was interrupted by opinions being sought from various other gods, by Horus and Seth engaging in

41. A relief scene from the drama of 'The Triumph of Horus over His Enemies' on the inner face of the girdle wall of the Ptolemaic temple of Horus at Edfu.

further conflicts, and by the quarrels of the Divine Council. At last the Council wrote to Osiris, who replied with the threat of his power as ruler of the dead, who feared neither god nor man, and who demanded justice for his son. Judgement was therefore given in favour of Horus, Seth became lord of the deserts, and Horus succeeded to the throne of his father.

Three main themes are contained in the myth of Osiris, which are political, agricultural and ritual and which serve to explain and justify particular historical events and the growth of certain beliefs and practices. In political terms the myth preserves some dim historical elements of a time during the Predynastic Period when Egypt was divided into two kingdoms of Upper and Lower Egypt, each with its own ruler. Perhaps Osiris represents an early king whose death led to war between the two kingdoms. This is, however, extremely uncertain, especially as evidence relating to this aspect of Osiris, as opposed to his role as a fertility god, is so meagre before the end of the Old Kingdom. What is more probably recalled in the myth with the conflict of Horus and Seth

42. A wooden plastered and painted djed-pillar. Late Period. From Saqqara. This sacred symbol of Osiris may originally have been a stick with ears of corn attached to it, but later on it represented the backbone of Osiris and was a sign of stability. (Bolton Museum, A.79.1969.)

is an early struggle between the two kingdoms in which the ruler of Lower Egypt (Horus being a local god from the Delta marshes) conquered the ruler of Upper Egypt (Seth being the local god of Ombos near Naqada). As a result the image of the falcon god Horus became a title applied to Egyptian rulers. However, later in the Predynastic Period it was a ruler of Upper Egypt who conquered Lower Egypt, uniting the two kingdoms into one state to found the First Dynasty.

In agricultural terms the death and resurrection of Osiris as a very early nature god were celebrated each year in simple popular ceremonies at the time of the Nile flood, when the seed crop was sown and when the harvest was gathered. In ritual terms the old agricultural ceremonies were joined with the cult of the dead to form the official Osirian rites and festivals. These were mainly performed at the places where parts of the body of Osiris were reputed to have been found or buried, which are recorded in an inscription at the late temple of Hathor at Dendera — at Athribis (heart), Busiris (backbone), Memphis (head), Abydos (head) and so on, some duplication being apparent. In late times the island of Bigah near Philae was another important place associated with Osiris. The festivals included 'mysteries', dramatic performances of episodes relating to the life, death and resurrection of Osiris, and often involved the planting of seed in Osiris-shaped moulds to germinate and grow by the end of the festival. These moulds on a smaller scale, filled with earth and grain, and having a similar function to corn dollies, are also found in tombs. They were symbols of the fact that Osiris brought life by growing food — 'the body of the god on whom one feeds', thus providing eternal sustenance and the hope of eternal life.

7
The individual's hope for eternity

Cemeteries of the Predynastic Period supply the earliest evidence for Egyptian funerary beliefs and customs. The dead were separated from the living not only by the fact of death, but also by being laid to rest in groups of graves at some distance from the towns and villages, on the edge of the desert. Within the grave the deceased was placed facing to the west and was accompanied by pottery vessels for food and drink, clothing, personal adornments and other goods. Grave contents varied in quantity and quality according to the status of the tomb owner. It is clear that to the ancient Egyptian death was not the end and that there was thought to be a life after death, for which certain provisions and preparations had to be made. Death was a state which obviously inspired fear. The living were aware that death would come and claim them and aware of the power of the dead in the hereafter. However, the dead were also afraid of the living, who might desecrate their tombs, destroy their bodies and thereby bring about the eternal annihilation of their identities. To attain the life after death the individual required a tomb, 'the house for eternity', the preservation of his body or some suitable substitute as his unique identity and material needs of food, drink and so on to ensure continued existence. As well as the physical provisions, certain moral and ethical standards had to be met in order to gain eternity.

In the Old Kingdom, when the cult of Re was prominent, the conception of the afterlife was solar, with a solar judgement of the dead. The deceased had to be judged as having lived according to the principles of Maat, the set order. The exact nature of the solar afterlife for the individual Egyptian is difficult to assess. The Pyramid Texts are concerned with the eternal life of the god-king and with the necessary rituals to enable him to join the gods and to travel in the boat of Re. By the end of the Old Kingdom the role of Osiris as ruler of the dead began to assume more significance. During the short period of political troubles between the Old and Middle Kingdoms solar and Osirian ideas of the afterlife were to some extent merged and there occurred a democratisation in funerary beliefs. Certain concepts, which previously had been connected only with the king, were universalised and became applicable to everyone. The dead king was identified with Osiris, but each individual who

43. An unfinished granite statue of Osiris, god of the dead, in the southern quarries at Aswan.

hoped for eternal resurrection was henceforth identified with Osiris and might place the title 'the Osiris' in front of his or her name in funerary inscriptions.

The judgement of the dead gradually came under the authority of Osiris, reaching its developed form by the New Kingdom. The trial took place in the Hall of Judgement before forty-two assessor gods. The deceased was brought in by Anubis and, turning to each of the gods in turn, he or she denied having committed a particular sin. The total of forty-two sins ranged from serious crimes like murder to minor wrongdoings like listening to gossip. The text of this Negative Confession was part of chapter 125 of the Book of the Dead. During the confession Anubis, using a balance scale, weighed the heart of the deceased against a feather, the symbol of Maat and therefore truth and order. The results were written down by Thoth. Nearby the Devourer, a composite monster with crocodile, lion and hippopotamus elements, waited hopefully in the event of the deceased failing the test. However, a successful outcome was apparently

44. A bronze *Ba* bird, the manifestation of the deceased on earth. Late Period. (Petrie Museum, UC.8188.)

virtually guaranteed and the deceased was thus declared to be 'true of voice' or 'justified'. The dead person was then taken by Horus and presented to Osiris, who was seated on his throne accompanied by Isis and Nephthys, and received his reward of admittance to the afterlife.

In addition to the physical needs and moral requirements for eternity, there were certain other concepts connected with the identity of the living and dead individual. A very early concept was that of the *Akh,* meaning glorified or transfigured spirit. From the First Dynasty this was a term applied to the dead. Through the preparation of his body for burial, the deceased had undergone *s'akhu* or glorification and was described as 'one who has gone to his *Akh'.* The dead as *Akhu* existed in the heaven as stars around the pole star and were therefore eternal and unchanging.

Another early concept was that of the *Ba,* which is usually translated as meaning the soul. Originally this quality was an

45. The false door from the tomb of Sennedjsui at Dendera. Ninth Dynasty. The false door communicated with the burial chamber in the tomb and bore inscriptions relating to offerings for the deceased and preserved his name and identity. (Bolton Museum, 56.98.35.)

attribute of the gods and then was assumed by the king. The quality of *Ba* or *Bau* was possessed by the king during his lifetime and refers to his power and renown. The king also had power when he died and therefore the *Ba* became connected with death in a somewhat different form and was linked with private individuals from the end of the Old Kingdom. It seems likely that *Ba* existed in the living individual but was released or separated from the body after death. It remained on earth as a manifestation of the deceased and was depicted as a bird with a human head. The home of the *Ba* was the body in the tomb, but it was able to go out freely and bring back life to the body and thus preserve the deceased's identity on earth.

A further concept was that of the *Ka,* which was inherent in gods, kings and men and which is perhaps best translated as meaning the life-force. The *Ka* came into existence at the moment of the individual's conception and was born with him. The creator god Khnum is often depicted modelling man and *Ka* together on his potter's wheel as though the *Ka* was a double or clone. The *Ka* remained an integral part of the individual during his lifetime but at death went on to some future existence. The funerary ceremonies, in particular the mummification and the ritual of the Opening of the Mouth to restore the living senses to the body, were designed to relink the man with his *Ka*. The deceased then became 'he who has gone to his *Ka*'. The ordinary individual possessed one *Ka,* the king had several and the gods had many. Re was credited with fourteen *Kas,* which in Ptolemaic times were applied to the god and the king and which were enumerated as strength, might, prosperity, food, veneration, eternity, radiance, glory, fame, magic, authority, sight, hearing and perception. These represent a summary of attributes, which were undoubtedly part of the concept as well as the notion of life-force. For the individual the *Ka* was not essentially eternal in the new life but needed to be sustained with offerings of food and drink and all good things. The funerary formula inscribed in tombs and on stelae invoked the king as owner of all to give offerings to a named god, so that the god could present the offerings to the *Ka* of the deceased.

Two more components were necessary for the deceased's well-being. The first of these was his heart, the source of thought and emotion and of life itself. Although the lungs were removed during mummification, the heart was left in the body for its crucial test in the judgement of the dead. From the New Kingdom onwards it was often protected with a large heart scarab,

46. The Stele of Iy, a sculptor, from tomb 321 at Abydos, excavated by John Garstang. Middle Kingdom. At the top of the stele are figures of Wepwawet, the jackal cemetery god closely associated with Osiris at Abydos. The stele also perpetuates the name of Iy and depicts the members of his family and household. (Bolton Museum, 10.20.11.)

inscribed with chapter 30 of the Book of the Dead, exhorting it to act as a true witness. After the judgement the heart was returned to the dead person for his continued life and from the Sixth Dynasty onwards its presence might be ensured by the provision of a heart amulet on the chest. The other necessary component was the deceased's name, which through its power could preserve life and identity. Tomb inscriptions, the coffin, statues, stelae and other grave goods therefore bore the name. If disaster struck and many of these things were destroyed, the name itself preserved in some form or other was sufficient for eternal survival.

The afterlife was imagined as continuing an existence on earth, as becoming one of the imperishable stars, as journeying across the heavens and eternal places with Re and as travelling through the Underworld with Osiris, a realm to which Re brought light and joy at night. Among these the Underworld was the great unknown and was therefore the dominant feature of funerary texts from the Middle Kingdom onwards. Identification with

47. Scenes of the Underworld from the tomb of Tuthmosis III in the Valley of the Kings, Thebes. Eighteenth Dynasty. (From J. Baikie, *A History of Egypt,* volume II, 1929.)

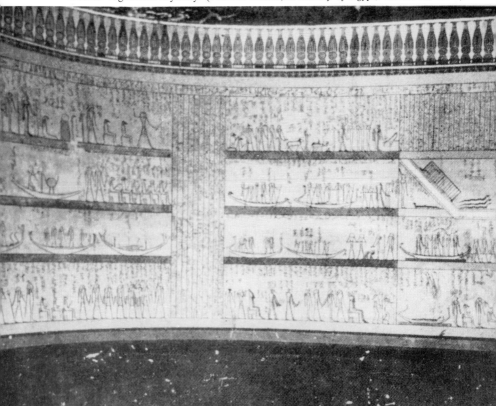

Osiris was a crucial factor both through the judgement after death and through association with his major cult centres. Of these the most important was Abydos and either the pilgrimage to Abydos was depicted on the walls of the tomb or the deceased erected a stele along the great processional way at Abydos which led to the tomb of Osiris. The so-called tomb of Osiris was actually the burial place of Djer, a long-forgotten king of the First Dynasty. From the Eleventh Dynasty, in the Coffin Texts and the Book of the Two Ways, the Underworld has become a realm with many dangers which must be conquered and which express the natural fear of death. The dangers became more numerous and terrible in the New Kingdom texts of the Book of Amduat and the Book of Gates, in which the Underworld was divided into twelve divisions, the hours of night.

Thus there was a confusing number of elements on earth, above it and below it which contributed to the afterlife, representing ideas which had been brought together over a long period of time. All of these were aspects of the afterlife. The deceased became part of the unchanging natural rhythm of the universe, the universe as he conceived it, encompassing the earth, the sky, the sun, the stars and the Underworld. All of these were places of the gods into which he was absorbed in a continuous journey of existence for as long as eternity might last.

8
Gods and goddesses: a glossary

Amun: originally a primeval god and later the god of Thebes. In human form he was a man with a tall plumed headdress. His sacred animals were the ram and the goose. From the New Kingdom identified with Re as Amun-Re.

Anubis: jackal god of embalming and of the dead and cemeteries, shown as a jackal or a jackal-headed man.

Apis: sacred bull, herald of the god Ptah of Memphis.

Apophis: serpent personification of darkness and enemy of the sun god, Re.

Aten: physical disk of the sun and an aspect of Re. Particularly worshipped in the Late Eighteenth Dynasty as a sun disk with rays ending in human hands and closely associated with the king Akhenaten. Main cult centre at Amarna.

Atum: primeval deity of Heliopolis and creator god, later identified with Re. Shown in human form.

Bastet: cat goddess of grace and joy, depicted as a cat or cat-headed woman. Her main cult centre was Bubastis.

Bes: dwarf of ugly appearance, a popular divinity who was a protector against evil.

Buchis: sacred bull, herald of the god Monthu at Armant.

Geb: the earth god, a man usually lying down.

Hapy: god of the Nile, a fertile man with a papyrus plant on his head.

Harakhty: the morning sun, Horus of the Horizon, frequently shown as a falcon-headed man.

Haroeris: aspect of Horus as Horus the Elder, a falcon deity and god of the king.

Harpocrates: aspect of Horus as the son of Osiris and Isis and therefore a child with the sidelock of youth.

Harsiesis: Horus as the son of Isis.

Hathor: cow goddess in animal, human or hybrid form, often as a woman with cow's ears. Her main cult centre was at Dendera.

Herishef: ram deity of Heracleopolis, who appears as a ram or a ram-headed man.

Horus: falcon sky god who became a deity of the sun and the king, and who was also later identified as the son of Osiris.

Isis: goddess in human form whose symbol was the throne as mother of Horus and the king, but she was also the sister-wife of Osiris and protector of the dead. She possessed great magical powers and later was very much connected with Hathor. Both goddesses could be shown wearing cow's horns and sun disks.

Khepri: the scarab beetle, creative form of the sun god Re, either as a scarab or a scarab-headed man.

Khnum: deity of Elephantine, a creator and potter god. His animal was the ram and he is depicted as a ram or a ram-headed man.

Khonsu: moon god of Thebes, child of Amun and Mut, who is either falcon-headed or has a moon disk on his head.

Maat: daughter goddess of Re, his divine order, a woman with her feather symbol on her head.

Min: god of fertility and of desert paths, with his cult centre at Coptos. His Predynastic sign was a thunderbolt, later depicted as a human ithyphallic figure and often identified with Amun.

Mnevis: sacred bull, herald of the god Re at Heliopolis.

Monthu: deity of Armant and then Thebes. Falcon-headed god of warfare.

Mut: goddess of Thebes, consort of Amun and mother of Khonsu. Shown as a woman with a vulture skin on her head or identified with a lioness, particularly as Sekhmet.

Nefertum: the divine lotus or a man with a lotus blossom on his head. Child of the sun and also the son of Ptah and Sekhmet at Memphis.

Neith: goddess of Sais and a divinity of warfare, with her early symbols of a bow and arrows and shield. Later as a protective goddess she guarded the dead with Isis, Nephthys and Selket.

Nephthys: sister-wife of Seth and sister of Isis and Osiris in the Heliopolitan ennead. She was a protector of the dead and is shown as a woman with her hieroglyphic sign on her head.

Nun: primordial deity of the waters of chaos, depicted in human form.

Nut: sky goddess, daughter of the air god Shu and wife of the earth god Geb. Represented either as a woman or as a cow.

Osiris: god of fertility and ruler of the dead, who is a mummiform figure with the attributes of a king. Principal cult centre at Abydos.

Ptah: god of Memphis, creator and deity of craftsmen, who appears like a primitive statue with a tight cap on his head and usually carries a sceptre.

Re: sun god with many forms, but often represented as the sun disk or as a falcon-headed man. His main cult centre was at Heliopolis.

Re-Harakhty: falcon-headed deity combining aspects of Re and Horus.

Sekhmet: lioness goddess of war as a lion-headed woman. At Memphis she was the wife of Ptah and mother of Nefertum and at Thebes was identified with the goddess Mut.

Selket: a goddess in human form with her symbol, the scorpion, on her head. She personified the sun's heat and was also a protector of the dead.

Seth: god of wind and storms, lord of the deserts and the enemy of Osiris and Horus. He could be depicted in a number of animal forms including the hippopotamus and the crocodile. As an animal-headed human figure, his sacred animal remains unidentified and could be mythical with its dog and antelope elements.

Shu: god of air, a man with a feather, his hieroglyphic sign, on his head, who separates earth and sky.

Sobek: crocodile deity of the Fayum and Kom Ombo, frequently represented as a crocodile-headed man.

Tatenen: primeval deity of Memphis, an earth god, later identified with Ptah.

Taurt: hippopotamus goddess, a popular divinity who helped women in childbirth and who was associated with domestic life.

Tefnut: goddess of moisture and sister-wife of the air god Shu.

Thoth: god of Hermopolis, creator, moon god, divinity of wisdom and scribe of the gods. His sacred animals were the ibis and the baboon and he could take the form of either animal, but is more generally shown as an ibis-headed man.

Wepwawet: jackal deity of Asyut, associated with warfare, but later mainly a guardian of the dead, connected with Osiris at Abydos.

9
Further reading

Clark, R. T. Rundle *Myth and Symbol in Ancient Egypt.* Thames and Hudson, London 1959, reprinted 1978.

Erman, A. *The Ancient Egyptians. A Sourcebook of their Writings.* Harper reprint, New York, 1966.

Frankfort, H. *Ancient Egyptian Religion.* Harper, New York, 1961.

Hornung, E. *Conceptions of God in Ancient Egypt.* Routledge and Kegan Paul, London, 1983.

James, T. G. H. (editor). *An Introduction to Ancient Egypt.* British Museum, London, 1978.

James, T. G. H. *Myths and Legends of Ancient Egypt.* Hamlyn, London, 1969.

Lichtheim, M. *Ancient Egyptian Literature* (two volumes). University of California Press, Berkeley, 1973 and 1975.

Lurker, M. *The Gods and Symbols of Ancient Egypt.* Thames and Hudson, London, 1980.

Shorter, A. W. *The Egyptian Gods.* Routledge and Kegan Paul, London, 1937, reprinted 1979.

Simpson, W. K. (editor). *The Literature of Ancient Egypt.* Yale University Press, New Haven, 1973.

10
Museums to visit

Museums with Egyptology collections include:

Ashmolean Museum of Art and Archaeology, Beaumont Street, Oxford OX1 2PH. Telephone: Oxford (0865) 512651.

Birmingham Museum and Art Gallery, Chamberlain Square, Birmingham B3 3DH. Telephone: 021-235 2834.

Bolton Museum and Art Gallery, Le Mans Crescent, Bolton, Lancashire BL1 1SA. Telephone: Bolton (0204) 22311 extension 379.

British Museum, Great Russell Street, London WC1B 3DG. Telephone: 01-636 1555 or 1558.

City of Bristol Museum and Art Gallery, Queens Road, Bristol, Avon BS8 1RL. Telephone: Bristol (0272) 299771.

Dundee Museums and Art Galleries, Albert Square, Dundee DD1 1DA. Telephone: Dundee (0382) 27643.

Durham University Oriental Museum, Elvet Hill, Durham DH1 3TH. Telephone: Durham (0385) 66711.

Fitzwilliam Museum, Trumpington Street, Cambridge CB2 1RB. Telephone: Cambridge (0223) 69501.
Glasgow Art Gallery and Museum, Kelvingrove, Glasgow G3 8AG. Telephone: 041-334 1134.
Leicestershire Museum and Art Gallery, New Walk, Leicester LE1 6TD. Telephone: Leicester (0533) 554100.
Manchester Museum, The University of Manchester, Oxford Road, Manchester M13 9PL. Telephone: 061-273 3333.
Merseyside County Museums, William Brown Street, Liverpool L3 8EN. Telephone: 051-207 0001 or 5451.
Petrie Museum of Egyptian Archaeology, University College London, Gower Street, London WC1E 6BT. Telephone: 01-387 7050 extension 617.
Plymouth City Museum and Art Gallery, Drake Circus, Plymouth, Devon PL4 8AJ. Telephone: Plymouth (0752) 668000 extension 4378.
Royal Museum of Scotland, Chambers Street, Edinburgh EH1 1JF. Telephone: 031-225 7534.

Acknowledgements

There are a number of people whom I would like to thank for their help in the preparation of this book, and particularly for assistance with the illustrations. The cover illustration is reproduced by courtesy of Towneley Hall Art Gallery and Museums and Burnley Borough Council. Photographs of objects in the Bolton Museum collection are reproduced by kind permission of Bolton Museums and Art Gallery and Bolton Metropolitan Borough Council. The reproduction of the bronze statue of Osiris, fig. 38, appears by courtesy of the Lady Lever Art Gallery, Port Sunlight, and Merseyside County Council. Other photographs were taken on a visit to Egypt in 1984 and thanks are due to Dr George Fildes, who having unfortunately lost his own camera through theft, took many excellent colour slides for us both with my camera, which I have been able to copy on to black and white film. The Petrie Museum of Egyptian Archaeology, Department of Egyptology, University College London, has generously allowed me to use photographs of a number of items in their collection and I express my thanks to the Curator, Barbara Adams, for providing me with the illustrations and for other help and support. Acknowledgement is also made to W. J. Murnane and Penguin Books for the Chronology reproduced here in an abbreviated form.